student WORKBOOK

AS/A2 English Literature
Unseen Examination Questions

Michael Fynes-Clinton

D1795349

Philip Allan Updates, an imprint of Hodder Education, part of Hachette Livre UK, Market Place, Deddington, Oxfordshire OX15 0SE

Orders

Bookpoint Ltd, 130 Milton Park, Abingdon, Oxfordshire OX14 4SB

tel: 01235 827720, fax: 01235 400454

e-mail: uk.orders@bookpoint.co.uk

Lines are open 9.00 a.m.–5.00 p.m., Monday to Saturday, with a 24-hour message answering service. You can also order through the Philip Allan Updates website: www.philipallan.co.uk

© Philip Allan Updates 2008

ISBN 978-1-84489-474-1

First printed 2008

Impression number 5 4 3 2 1

Year 2013 2012 2011 2010 2009 2008

Printed in Spain

Hachette Livre UK's policy is to use papers that are natural, renewable and recyclable products and made from wood grown in sustainable forests. The logging and manufacturing processes are expected to conform to the environmental regulations of the country of origin.

P01281

Introduction

This is one of a series of workbooks which focus on different aspects of AS and A2 courses in English literature regardless of which specification you are following. This workbook looks at how to answer the unseen questions which appear as part of many examinations.

All the awarding bodies have introduced new specifications to be taught from September 2008 and first examined in 2009. This workbook is relevant to both old and new specifications.

The workbook is divided into several parts. After a brief initial section designed to encourage you to think about literature in general, there are three central sections which focus on the detail of literary analysis. The next section is about the process of answering the question — through annotating the passage(s) to structuring your answer. Some notes on comparisons between passages and the role of wider reading are given at the end of this section. A number of passages (both prose and poetry) are then offered for practice, followed by a list of useful critical terms that have not already been introduced. The workbook finishes with a section on examinations and assessment.

A selection of poems and prose extracts are included in the workbook. You can use these in any way that is useful and in any order. If the specification that you are following requires comparisons, then there is scope for this.

You can use this workbook in a variety of ways. It provides a useful grounding for your AS year or alternatively it can play a significant part in the way you respond to the demands of A2. The book is designed to be used either on your own at home or with others in the classroom as a focus for group discussion. The best way is probably a combination of the two.

Unseen examinations are a part of many of the new specifications; this is because they can be used to assess many aspects of your literary understanding and also your ability to respond confidently in examination conditions. To achieve a high grade, you need to do more than identify and comment briefly on literary features. Analysis is a complex process which starts with the ability to focus and prioritise your thoughts on reading a poem or passage for the first time. When you find you can do this confidently, the actual writing of the response should come easily with practice.

Ideas about literature

1 Read the following comments on literature carefully. Discuss them in small groups, deciding first of all what each writer means and then whether you agree or disagree with what has been said. Keep careful notes of your discussions.

On writing in general or prose texts

> Writing is like driving at night in the fog. You can only see as far as your headlights, but you can make the whole trip that way.
>
> E. L. Doctorow, *Writers at Work*, 8th series, ed. G. Plimpton (1988)

> Successful imaginary worlds ask complex questions about identity and moral choice.
>
> Amanda Craig, *The Times* (17 November 2007)

> 1) Novels are things to be enjoyed; 2) the better we read them, the more enjoyment we will derive from them.
>
> John Sutherland, *How to Read a Novel* (2006)

....

....

....

....

....

....

....

....

....

On poetry in particular

This is the way William Carlos Williams started his long poem *Paterson*, stressing that, as a writer, he started from the world which we experience around us every day:

> To make a start,
> out of particulars
> and make them general
>
> William Carlos Williams, *Paterson* (1958)

Another writer who often wrote about the way poetry can enhance the ordinary world that we live in, and the way writing structures and moulds our ordinary experience, was the poet Philip Larkin. As he said:

> Writing poetry is playing off the natural rhythms and word order of speech against the artificialities of rhyme and metre.
>
> Philip Larkin, interviewed in 1982 in P. Gourevitch (ed.), *Paris Review Interviews*, Vol. 2 (republished 2007)

Here are some further observations by Robert Lowell and Carl Sandburg.

> You may feel the doorknob more strongly than some big personal event, and the doorknob will open into something that you can use as your own... Often images and often the sense of the beginning and end of a poem are all you have — some journey to be gone through between those things... Then the great moment comes when there's enough resolution of your technical equipment, your way of constructing things, and what you can make a poem out of it, to hit something you really want to say.
>
> Robert Lowell, American poet, interviewed in 1961 in P. Gourevitch (ed.), *Paris Review Interviews*, Vol. 2 (republished 2007)

> Poetry is the opening and closing of a door, leaving those who look through to guess what is seen during a moment.
>
> Carl Sandburg, *Good Morning, America* (1928)

Starting the unseen task

What are you looking for in prose and poetry?

There are a number of different ways in which examiners ask you to respond to unseen passages. In some cases, the focus is on individual poems or prose extracts, but sometimes you are asked to compare passages, and with some specifications, the comparison involves texts you have already prepared. In most cases, the unseen question is an open one (which might ask you to write about language, form and structure, for example). On the positive side, this gives you many opportunities to explore the passage as *you* want to, but, less happily perhaps, does not provide you with a clear focus for your answer.

It is therefore crucial to have practised two particular aspects of the task: how you choose the important words/phrases/lines in an unseen text and how you organise your response.

In this section, we look briefly at how you know what to look for in an unseen question. In other words, what is worth writing about?

Here are some preliminary ideas for you to consider:
- What is the passage actually about? Do not be afraid to start with the obvious. For example, if there is a title, what does it tell you?
- What do you think the writer's attitude to the material is? Is there a clear agenda or message?
- What seems to be the focus of the passage? What particular details of place, character (or anything else) are particularly mentioned or described?
- Are there any obvious ideas which the writer is trying to explore?
- Which words 'jump off the page'? To be able to identify these is a particularly crucial aspect of making an appropriate response to an unseen passage. Some students waste their time by focusing on elements in the passage about which there is not much to say, ignoring other elements which might show more clearly their ability to analyse.
- Can you see a pattern in the way the language is used or in the development of the ideas?
- Can you detect a structure or organisation underpinning the poem or passage?

1 Here are a few prose passages, poems or parts of poems. In each case, highlight what you think is important, using the list above, or perhaps thinking of other aspects not included in the list. Then discuss your choices in small groups, identifying clearly why you have chosen those particular aspects.

> Is this a holy thing to see,
> In a rich and fruitful land,
> Babes reduc'd to misery,
> Fed with cold and usurous hand?
>
> Is that trembling cry a song?
> Can it be a song of joy?
> And so many children poor?
> It is a land of poverty!
>
> And their sun does never shine.
> And their fields are bleak & bare.
> And their ways are filled with thorns
> It is eternal winter there.
>
> For where-e'er the sun does shine,
> And where-e'er the rain does fall:
> Babes can never hunger there,
> Nor poverty the mind appall.
>
> William Blake, 'Holy Thursday' (1793, from *Songs of Innocence and Experience*, 1789–94)

They walked on, for some time, through the most crowded and densely inhabited part of the town; and then, striking down a narrow street more dirty and miserable than any they had yet passed through, paused to look for the house which was the object of their search. The houses on either side were high and large, but very old, and tenanted by people of the poorest class: as their neglected appearance would have sufficiently denoted, without the concurrent testimony afforded by the squalid looks of the few men and women who, with folded arms and bodies half doubled, occasionally skulked along. A great many of the tenements had shop-fronts; but these were fast closed, and mouldering away; only the upper rooms being inhabited. Some houses which had become insecure from age and decay, were prevented from falling into the street, by huge beams of wood reared against the walls, and firmly planted in the road; but even these crazy dens seemed to have been selected as the nightly haunts of some houseless wretches, for many of the rough boards which supplied the place of door and window, were wrenched from their positions, to afford an aperture wide enough for the passage of a human body. The kennel was stagnant and filthy. The very rats, which were here and there lay putrefying in its rottenness, were hideous with famine.

Charles Dickens, *Oliver Twist* (1838)

Not seldom from the uproar I retired
Into a silent bay, or sportively
Glanced sideway, leaving the tumultuous throng,
To cut across the image of a star
That gleam'd upon the ice: and oftentimes
When we had given our bodies to the wind,
And all the shadowy banks, on either side,
Came sweeping through the darkness, spinning still
The rapid line of motion; then at once
Have I, reclining back upon my heels,
Stopp'd short, yet still the solitary cliffs
Wheeled by me — even as if the earth had roll'd
With visible motion her diurnal round!
Behind me did they stretch in solemn train
Feebler and feebler, and I stood and watch'd
Till all was tranquil as a dreamless sleep.

William Wordsworth, *The Prelude*, Book 1 (1805–06 version)

Grandfather's skirts would flap in the wind along the churchyard path and I would hang on. He often found things to do in the vestry, excuses for getting out of the vicarage (kicking the swollen door, cursing) and so long as he took me he couldn't get up to much. I was a sort of hobble; he was my minder and I was his. He'd have liked to get further away, but petrol was rationed. The church was at least safe. My grandmother never went near it — except feet first in her coffin, but that was years later, when she was buried in the same grave with him. Rotting together for eternity, one flesh at the last after a lifetime's mutual loathing. In life, though, she never invaded his patch; once inside the churchyard gate he was on his own ground, in his element. He was good at funerals, being gaunt and lined, marked with mortality. He had a scar down his hollow cheek too, which Grandma had done with the carving knife one of the many times he came home pissed and incapable.

Lorna Sage, *Bad Blood* (2000)

But in the course of that survey her eyes met Deronda's, and instead of averting them as she would have desired to do, she was unpleasantly conscious that they were arrested — how long? The darting sense that he was measuring her and looking down on her as an inferior, that he was of different quality from the human dross around her, that he felt himself in a region outside and above her, and was examining her as specimen of a lower order, roused a tingling resentment which stretched the moment with conflict. It did not bring the blood to her cheeks, but sent it away from her lips. She controlled herself by the help of an inward defiance, and without other sign of emotion than this lip-paleness turned to her play.

George Eliot, *Daniel Deronda* (1876)

The language of prose and poetry

Any passage that you are likely to be looking at as an unseen will probably contain more than one type of language. Although it may appear to be rather an artificial task to break up the language in a piece of writing into types, it does allow you to focus on literary techniques — how writers create an impact on their readers.

1 For each of these passages, highlight the words and phrases which 'jump off the page' and then identify the type(s) of language that they seem to be. In other words, what kind of 'job' are they doing? Here is a list of possible types:

- Language which describes the physical world around us.
- Language which explores character.
- Language which describes action.
- Language which develops and analyses ideas.
- Language which reflects the writer's state of mind.

The sun had not yet risen. The sea was indistinguishable from the sky, except that the sea was slightly creased as if a cloth had wrinkles in it. Gradually as the sky whitened a dark line lay on the horizon dividing the sea from the sky and the grey cloth became barred with thick strokes moving, one after another, beneath the surface, following each other, pursuing each other, perpetually.

As they neared the shore each bar rose, heaped itself, broke and swept a thin veil of white water across the sand. The wave paused, and then drew out again, sighing like a sleeper whose breath comes and goes unconsciously. Gradually the dark bar on the horizon became clear as if the sediment in an old wine-bottle had sunk and left the glass green. Behind it, too, the sky cleared as if the white sediment there had sunk, or as if the arm of a woman couched beneath the horizon had raised a lamp and flat bars of white, green and yellow spread across the sky like the blades of a fan. Then she raised her lamp higher and the air seemed to become fibrous and to tear away from the green surface flickering and flaming in red and yellow fibres like the smoky fire that roars from a bonfire. Gradually the fibres of the burning bonfire were fused into one haze, one incandescence which lifted the weight of the woollen grey sky on top of it and turned it to a million atoms of soft blue. The surface of the sea slowly became transparent and lay rippling and sparkling until the dark stripes were almost rubbed out. Slowly the arm that held the lamp raised it higher and then higher until a broad flame became visible; an arc of fire burnt on the rim of the horizon, and all round it the sea blazed gold.

The light struck upon the trees in the garden, making one leaf transparent and then another. One bird chirped high up; there was a pause; another chirped lower down. The sun sharpened the walls of the house, and rested like the tip of a fan upon a white blind and made a blue finger-print of shadow under the leaf by the bedroom window. The blind stirred slightly, but all within was dim and unsubstantial. The birds sang their blank melody outside.

Virginia Woolf, *The Waves* (1931)

(Continued overleaf)

Again they were stumbling across the field. He felt the pain in his side like a flash of colour. The boy was in his arms and again the woman seemed to be dragging back, and trying to get her son from him. There were hundreds in the field now, all making for the woods on the far side. At the shrill whine of the bomb everyone cowered on the ground. But the woman had no instinct for danger and he had to pull her down again. This time they were pressing their faces into freshly turned earth. As the screech grew louder the woman shouted what sounded like a prayer. He realised then that she wasn't speaking French. The explosion was on the far side of the road, more than a hundred and fifty yards away. But now the first Stuka was turning over the village and dropping for the strafe. The boy had gone silent with shock. His mother wouldn't stand. Turner pointed to the Stuka coming in over the rooftops. They were right in its path and there was no time for argument. She wouldn't move. He threw himself down into the furrow. The rippling thuds of machine gun fire in the ploughed earth and the engine roar flashed past them. A wounded soldier was screaming. Turner was on his feet. But the woman would not take his hand. She sat on the ground and hugged the boy tightly to her.

Ian McEwan, *Atonement* (2001)

Rain, midnight rain, nothing but the wild rain
On this bleak hut, and solitude, and me
Remembering again that I shall die
And neither hear the rain nor give it thanks
For washing me cleaner than I have been
Since I was born into this solitude.
Blessed are the dead that the rain rains upon:
But here I pray that none whom once I loved
Is dying tonight or lying still awake
Solitary, listening to the rain,
Either in pain or thus in sympathy
Helpless among the living and the dead,
Like a cold water among broken reeds,
Myriads of broken reeds all still and stiff,
Like me who have no love which this wild rain
Has not dissolved except the love of death,
If love it be for what is perfect and
Cannot, the tempest tells me, disappoint.

Edward Thomas, 'Rain' (1917)

The Frost performs its secret ministry,
Unhelped by any wind. The owlet's cry
Came loud — and hark, again! loud as before.
The inmates of my cottage, all at rest,
Have left me to that solitude, which suits
Abstruser musings : save that at my side
My cradled infant slumbers peacefully.
'Tis calm indeed! so calm, that it disturbs
And vexes meditation with its strange
And extreme silentness. Sea, hill, and wood,
This populous village! Sea, and hill, and wood,
With all the numberless goings-on of life,
Inaudible as dreams! the thin blue flame
Lies on my low-burnt fire, and quivers not;
Only that film, which fluttered on the grate,
Still flutters there, the sole unquiet thing.
Methinks, its motion in this hush of nature
Gives it dim sympathies with me who live,
Making it a companionable form,
Whose puny flaps and freaks the idling Spirit
By its own moods interprets, every where
Echo or mirror seeking of itself,
And makes a toy of Thought.

Samuel Taylor Coleridge, from 'Frost at Midnight' (1798)

If one wanted to show a foreigner England, perhaps the wisest course would be to take him to the final section of the Purbeck Hills, and stand him on their summit, a few miles to the east of Corfe. Then system after system of our island would roll together under his feet. Beneath him is the valley of the Frome, and all the wild lands that come tossing down from Dorchester, black and gold, to mirror their gorse in the expanses of Poole. The valley of the Stour is beyond, unaccountable stream, dirty at Blandford, pure at Wimborne — the Stour, sliding out of fat fields, to marry the Avon beneath the tower of Christchurch. The valley of the Avon — invisible, but far to the north the trained eye may see Clearbury Ring that guards it, and the imagination may leap beyond that on to Salisbury Plain itself, and beyond the Plain to all the glorious downs of Central England. Nor is Suburbia absent. Bournemouth's ignoble coast cowers to the right, heralding the pine-trees that mean, for all their beauty, red houses, and the Stock Exchange, and extend to the gates of London itself. So tremendous is the City's trail! But the cliffs of Freshwater it shall never touch, and the island will guard the Island's purity till the end of time. Seen from the west, the Wight is beautiful beyond all laws of beauty. It is as if a fragment of England floated forward to greet the foreigner — chalk of our chalk, turf of our turf, epitome of what will follow. And behind the fragment lies Southampton, hostess to the nations, and Portsmouth, a latent fire, and all around it, with double and treble collision of tides, swirls the sea. How many villages appear in this view! How many castles! How many churches, vanished or triumphant! How many ships, railways, and roads! What incredible variety of men working beneath that lucent sky to what final end! The reason fails, like a wave on the Swanage beach; the imagination swells, spreads, and deepens, until it becomes geographic and encircles England.

E. M. Forster, *Howard's End* (1910)

2 Look back over the notes you have made on the poem and prose extracts on pages 9–14. In each case, develop your ideas in more detail, identifying clearly the effect of the words. For example, they might have made you think about something, explored the way in which people respond in particular situations, described the natural environment in detail and so on. Continue on a separate sheet of paper if necessary.

Developing the detail: prose and poetry

Figurative language

One of the most common aspects of literary language in unseen passages is figurative language. This is a general term for imagery, used by writers to create a particular impact through intensity of description. You are probably familiar with metaphors (when two things which are in some ways quite different are used to bring out their similarities, perhaps in a rather unusual way that is not literally true, for example 'the sea gnawed at the cliffs.'). You are also probably used to similes (similarities are expressed through a comparison introduced by 'like' or 'as'). Metaphors and similes are types of imagery.

One general aspect of figurative language is the way it often suggests or refers to a meaning beyond the most obvious. In this way it relates to the subtext of the passage and might prompt you to comment on a pattern created through the various images in the poem or prose extract.

1 Read the following short extracts from poems, all of which use natural imagery in some way. In each case write careful notes about how the extracts use imagery, focusing on particular words and details.

> The swallows are italic again,
> cutting their sky-jive
> between the telephone wires
>
> Owen Sheers, from 'Swallows' (2005)

Outside the green velvet sitting room
white roses bloom after rain.
They hold water and sunlight
like cups of fine white china.

Gillian Clarke, from 'White Roses' (1997)

Through the brunt wind that dented the balls of my eyes
The tent of the hills drummed and strained its guyrope,

The fields quivering, the skyline a grimace,
At any second to bang and vanish with a flap:
The wind flung a magpie away and a black-
Back gull bent like an iron bar slowly.

Ted Hughes, from 'Wind' (1957)

The meaningless plungings of water and the wind,
Theatrical distances, bronze shadows heaped
On high horizons, mountainous atmospheres
Of sky and sea.

Wallace Stevens, from 'The Idea of Order at Key West' (1936)

The winter evening settles down
With smell of steaks in passageways.
Six o'clock.
The burnt-out ends of smoky days.
And now a gusty shower wraps
The grimy scraps
Of withered leaves about your feet
And newspapers from vacant lots;
The showers beat
On broken blinds and chimneypots,
And at the corner of the street
A lonely cab-horse steams and stamps.
And then the lighting of the lamps.

T. S. Eliot, from 'Preludes' (1917)

I listened in emptiness on the moor-ridge.
The curlew's tear turned its edge on the silence.

Slowly detail leafed from the darkness. Then the sun
Orange, red, red erupted

Silently, and splitting to its core tore and flung cloud,
Shook the gulf open, showed blue,

And the big planets hanging —

Ted Hughes, from 'The Horses' (1957)

Prose description

2 Read the following prose extract, which comes at the start of the last novel Dickens published in his lifetime. Although there may be no specific examples of imagery which 'jump off the page', as with the poetry extracts above, the detail of the passage builds up a sense of atmosphere which creates an effective opening to the novel. Make careful notes on the ways in which Dickens does this, looking particularly at place and character.

The figures in this boat were those of a strong man with ragged grizzled hair and a sun-browned face, and a dark girl of nineteen or twenty, sufficiently like him to be recognizable as his daughter. The girl rowed, pulling a pair of sculls very easily; the man, with the rudder-lines slack in his hands, and his hands loose in his waistband, kept an eager look out. He had no net, hook, or line, and he could not be a fisherman; his boat had no cushion for a sitter, no paint, no inscription, no appliance beyond a rusty boathook and a coil of rope, and he could not be a waterman; his boat was too crazy and too small to take in cargo for delivery, and he could not be a lighterman or river-carrier; there was no clue to what he looked for, but he looked for something, with a most intent and searching gaze. The tide, which had turned an hour before, was running down, and his eyes watched every little race and eddy in its broad sweep, as the boat made slight head-way against it, or drove stern foremost before it, according as he directed his daughter by a movement of his head. She watched his face as earnestly as he watched the river. But, in the intensity of her look there was a touch of dread or horror.

Charles Dickens, *Our Mutual Friend* (1864–65)

Further ways to explore unseen passages: some key aspects of analysis

The main focus for assessment with unseen questions is, in general terms, your analysis of language, form and structure. So far, we have explored general questions to ask about an unseen passage and looked at different types of language, including imagery.

Here are a few notes on some of the other detailed aspects of prose and poetry which can help you to respond to an unseen text with confidence. It does not pretend to include everything you might need to know, nor should it be seen in any way as a checklist, as so much depends on the passage itself. You can also use the key terms list (pages 43–44) for explanations of other important aspects of literary analysis which you might find useful.

- **Subject, content, themes.** It is important to recognise the difference between these terms. The subject of any writing means what it says — the basic material, often implied by the title. The content refers in a more detailed way to this basic subject. Finally, the writer will adopt a particular approach to the content, following specific lines of thought; these are the themes.
- **Development of themes.** The idea of development is important. In all but the most simplistic writing, authors do not simply present an idea (through imagery, character etc.); they explore it from different perspectives, create ambiguities and ironies and let the reader understand its complexities. Even in a short extract or a poem, the central idea(s) develop and change, and you need to be aware of this.
- **Tone.** An understanding of tone is particularly important, as it reflects the attitude to the material adopted by the writer. For example, while satire may be the genre, the tone could be described as 'bitter' or 'angry'. It is also important that you realise that one tone is not necessarily set for the whole of a work, as even in quite a short poem it can change.
- **Genre and conventions.** The genre (or type) of a piece of writing in many ways controls our response to the material and our expectations when reading it. Generic conventions in this sense are not to be dismissed as 'conventional' but as the tools which a writer uses when writing in a particular style. For example, a genre may work with the convention of identifiable character types or a particular sort of ending.
- **Form and structure.** *Form* is the way in which the organisation of the words/poetic lines/action and so on reflect the demands of the genre and the subject matter. The *structure* of a poem or prose extract, however, is the way the ideas/narrative/ imagery and so on are organised in response to the needs of a particular piece of writing. In other words, the writer may have decided to use a particular form (recognisable through certain literary conventions) to express relevant ideas, but these ideas are structured through, for example, a descriptive opening, a sudden moment of shocking action and a concluding, quieter section which meditates on what has occurred.

- **Voice, persona, narrator, point of view.** The 'voice' in a piece of writing is a useful starting point from which to discuss a range of different literary aspects. The voice can be that of a first person narrator in a novel, or a persona in a poem — a created 'voice' that stands between the writer and the reader. In each case, this particular fictional creation 'mediates' our experience by judging or commenting on character, action and so on. This enables the writer to 'hide behind' the voice and manipulate the reader, often in quite complex ways. However, you should also remember that the 'voice' of a piece of writing can be unmediated — just the writer telling us how it is

- **Rhyme.** The important point to remember about rhyme is that your comments need to be related to other aspects of the poem/passage — for example, the particular impact on the reader or the way the rhyme is related to meaning or genre. To state simply that a particular rhyme scheme is used (aa, bb, c for example) is not, in itself, useful.

- **Irony, ambiguity, subtext.** It can be a mistake to go looking for 'hidden meanings' (subtext), but it is also true that the language of literature often contains a range of meanings, suggestions and resonances which other forms of writing lack. Likewise, writers can play on ambiguity to prompt us to think, or perhaps to deny us easy answers and assumptions — or even just to surprise us. In the case of irony, the writer can ensure that the reader establishes a distance from a character and perhaps is led to judge that character's actions.

- **Symbolism.** A symbol, in the simplest terms, is a word or phrase which refers to something beyond its basic meaning. It is both literally what it says it is (the sea, for instance) and also suggests something else (a sense of fate or the power of nature, for example). In this case the relationship is quite vague, but it can be a specific connection, and indeed some conventional symbols are part of our everyday lives (like flags). In unseen exams, symbols are important because they are part of the meaning of the passage, often related to other words or phrases, creating resonances through both the associations that readers make and as a result of the particular intentions of the writer.

- **Attitudes and values.** This is a useful phrase to use when exploring meaning, particularly when the question asks you to relate your understanding of a passage to your own wider reading in a theme or period, or to answer a question about the degree to which a passage is 'typical' of a certain type of writing. All writing to some degree reflects this sort of context. In the case of an unseen text when the point is not your own knowledge of the context, your response should be through the language, and in particular the tone of the writing. What is the relationship between the writer and the subject matter, and how does this reflect the writer's values and judgements?

- **The particular and the general.** One of the useful ways of analysing a passage is to look at the way it moves between particularity (identifying place, period, etc.), which gives us as readers a sense of identification and visualisation, and the universal (through themes and ideas), which is not confined by the specifics of detail.

- **Register.** The register of a piece of writing refers to the relationship between the chosen vocabulary and the purpose or genre. Sometimes a writer will shock us by breaking out of an accepted or conventional register so as to prompt us to think more clearly about a particular event, character or theme.

3 Go back to earlier passages (or choose from the practice texts on pages 33–42) and analyse them carefully, using some of the literary aspects described above.

Annotating and structuring

How to annotate a passage

In the examination you will have comparatively little time to annotate the passage(s), but practice will enable you to do this quickly. The aim of annotation is to:

- focus your attention on the key passages — these could be single words, phrases, a poetic line or two, a stanza, the beginning of an extract, and so on
- make clear any patterns that might emerge from your highlighting of key passages; these relationships between words and phrases might focus on the development of meaning or theme, or on a pattern of images or on other aspects of language use which create a particular effect or impact
- suggest ways that you might structure your answer, through focusing on possible key sources for your own analysis

There are several ways to annotate passages, but the key point is that you are able to complete all of the above quickly. In other words, highlights (useful as a preliminary brainstorm and as a guide to key passages), connections and the marginal notes. Although your specification may require you to make comparisons or refer to additional wider reading texts, in this activity we concentrate on annotating single passages so that you can practise the basic techniques involved.

1 Here is an example of a poem with some of the words and phrases highlighted. First, go through the passage and see if there are any other words that you think should be highlighted. Then, for each highlighted phrase or word, make some notes on its importance, remembering to make connections between them if that is appropriate.

I met a traveler from an antique land
Who said: Two vast and **trunkless** legs of stone
Stand in the desert. Near them, on the sand,
Half sunk, a **shattered visage** lies, whose frown,
And wrinkled lip, and **sneer of cold command**
Tell that its sculptor well those passions read
Which yet survive, stamped on **these lifeless things**,
The hand that mocked them, and the heart that fed.
And on the pedestal these words appear:
'My name is Ozymandias, king of kings:
Look on my works, ye Mighty, and despair!'
Nothing beside remains. Round the decay
Of that colossal wreck, boundless and bare
The lone and level sands stretch far away.

Percy Bysshe Shelley, 'Ozymandias' (1818)

2 Annotate the following prose passage as clearly as you can. When you have completed this, list the key aspects you have annotated using a series of bullet points. The central point is: what are the really important things to mention in any commentary on this passage?

The beauty of the night made him want to shout. A half-moon, dusky gold, was sinking behind the black sycamore at the end of the garden, making the sky dull purple with its glow. Nearer, a dim white fence of lilies went across the garden, and the air all round seemed to stir with scent, as if it were alive. He went across the bed of pinks, whose keen perfume came sharply across the rocking, heavy scent of the lilies, and stood alongside the white barrier of flowers. They flagged all loose, as if they were panting. The scent made him drunk. He went down to the field to watch the moon sink under.

A corncrake in the hay-close called insistently. The moon slid quite quickly downwards, growing more flushed. Behind him the great flowers leaned as if they were calling. And then, like a shock, he caught another perfume, something raw and coarse. Hunting round, he found the purple iris, touched their fleshy throats and their dark, grasping hands. At any rate, he had found something. They stood stiff in the darkness. Their scent was brutal. The moon was melting down upon the crest of the hill. It was gone; all was dark. The corncrake called still.

D. H. Lawrence, *Sons and Lovers* (1913)

_____
_____
_____
_____
_____
_____

How to structure an answer

When you have worked on the passage, annotating it as explained above, you still have one more thing to do before you start to write: you must structure your answer. If you leave out this stage your answer may simply be a list of the things that you picked on when you were annotating. This approach, largely a sequential commentary on the unseen passage(s), will not allow you to show that you can really focus on the important aspects and develop a close analysis, in which you relate meaning and language.

If you are responding to a single passage, the easiest way to structure an answer is to pick out the five or six aspects which stand out as the most important, and use them as the basis for your paragraphing.

Here are some examples:
- the opening or ending of the poem (of course, it needs to be a complete work for this to be a relevant focus)
- changes in tone or mood
- a developed theme
- the voice of the poem/extract
- a central opposition or contrast
- an image pattern (not just a single image)

As you annotate the passage/poem in the examination, you should get used to thinking of key aspects as you go along and make quick notes to return to when you come to structure your answer.

3 On pages 30 and 31 are two poems about love. Go through each one carefully, first annotating in the way we have discussed and then developing a list of five or six key aspects. At this point it would be useful to discuss your ideas with others in a small group. Finally, write a response, either to one of the poems or a comparison between them (depending upon what your specification requires you to do). You may decide to write this in timed conditions; if you do, remember to keep strictly to the time — there is not much point otherwise!

I ne'er was struck before that hour
With love so sudden and so sweet,
Her face it bloomed like a sweet flower
And stole my heart away complete.
My face turned pale as deadly pale.
My legs refused to walk away,
And when she looked, what could I ail?
My life and all seemed turned to clay.

And then my blood rushed to my face
And took my eyesight quite away,
The trees and bushes round the place
Seemed midnight at noonday.
I could not see a single thing,
Words from my eyes did start —
They spoke as chords do from the string,
And blood burnt round my heart.

Are flowers the winter's choice?
Is love's bed always snow?
She seemed to hear my silent voice,
Not love's appeal to know.
I never saw so sweet a face
As that I stood before.
My heart has left its dwelling-place
And can return no more.

John Clare, 'First Love' (undated)

O me, what eyes hath love put in my head,
Which have no correspondence with true sight,
Or if they have, where is my judgement fled
That censures falsely what they see aright?
If that be fair whereon my false eyes dote,
What means the world to say it is not so?
If it be not, then love doth well denote
Love's eye is not so true as all men's 'No.'
How can it? O, how can love's eye be true,
That is so vexed with watching and with tears?
No marvel then though I mistake my view:
The sun itself sees not till heaven clears.
O cunning love, with tears thou keep'st me blind,
Lest eyes well-seeing thy foul faults should find.

Shakespeare, Sonnet 148 (1609)

Comparisons and wider reading

Some of the new specifications ask you to respond to unseen passages in slightly different ways. Comparisons are central to many new specifications and it is not surprising, therefore, that the unseen question often requires you to develop a relationship between passages or to make connections with material you have already prepared.

Comparisons between passages

When you are making comparisons between passages, the same basic techniques of annotation apply. The examiner will not just have thrown two passages together at random; the connection is likely to be through an overall theme (such as love) with which you will already be familiar. You can, therefore, develop likely connections through literary approach, technique and theme before the examination. As you annotate the passages, ways of linking the two should become clear and these will provide your paragraph headings. It is important to remember that a comparison means what it says; the examiner does not want you to write separate blocks of commentary on each passage. What is needed is an analysis which draws the two together using some of the key aspects mentioned earlier in this workbook.

Use of prepared texts/wider reading

If you have studied a text which you are required to relate to an unseen passage, you will have in your mind a number of aspects of the text which could provide links. A theme like 'nature', for example, or the way the writer uses imagery. In the examination, your annotation of the unseen text should reveal a number of these familiar and prepared aspects, which should then provide a structure for your response.

If you are asked to relate a passage to your wider reading, it is important that you remember the golden rules when answering any question which involves reading of your own choice.
- Do not make the mistake of reading too much.
- Keep a clear log of your reading, with an indication for each passage about how you would use it.

Ask yourself: in what ways is the poem (for example) 'typical' of your choice of topic or theme? If you do this carefully, you should be confident about making links when you see the unseen.

Passages for practice

A number of passages are provided in this section for you to use as unseen texts. You may also wish to use some of the texts that you looked at in previous activities. The passages in this section are divided into poetry and prose and you may wish to treat them as single unseens, or to compare them if your specification requires you to do so in the examination. You will need to use additional sheets of paper for your notes and essays.

The way the examination questions are expressed can differ. For example:
- Write a critical commentary on…
- Write about the form, structure and language of…
- Compare the form, structure and language of…
- Comment on… (identified key features such as rhyme, imagery, dialogue)

Poetry passages

When I have fears that I may cease to be
Before my pen has glean'd my teeming brain,
Before high-piled books in charactery,
Hold like rich garners the full ripen'd grain;
When I behold upon the night's starr'd face
Huge cloudy symbols of a high romance,
And think that I may never live to trace
Their shadows, with the magic hand of chance;
And when I feel, fair creature of an hour,
That I shall never look upon thee more,
Never have relish in the faery power
Of unreflecting love; — then on the shore
    Of the wide world I stand alone, and think
    Till love and fame to nothingness do sink.

John Keats, 'When I have fears that I may cease to be' (1848)

Men heard this roar of parleying starlings, saw,
A thousand years ago even as now,
Black rooks with white gulls following the plough
So that the first are last until a caw
Commands that last are first again, — a law
Which was of old when one, like me, dreamed how
A thousand years might dust lie on his brow
Yet thus would birds do between hedge and shaw.
Time swims before me, making as a day
A thousand years, while the broad ploughland oak
Roars mill-like and men strike and bear the stroke
Of war as ever, audacious or resigned,
And God still sits aloft in the array
That we have wrought him, stone-deaf and stone-blind.

Edward Thomas, 'February Afternoon' (1916)

I heard a fly buzz when I died;
The stillness in the room
Was like the stillness in the air
Between the heaves of storm.

The eyes around had wrung them dry
And breaths were gathering firm
For that last onset, when the king
Be witnessed in the room.

I willed my keepsakes, signed away
What portion of me be
Assignable, and then 'it was'
There interposed a fly,

With blue, uncertain, stumbling buzz,
Between the light and me;
And then the windows failed, and then
I could not see to see.

Emily Dickinson, 'I heard a fly buzz when I died' (1896)

Marke but this flea, and marke in this,
How little that which thou deny'st me is;
Me it suck'd first, and now sucks thee,
And in this flea our two bloods mingled bee;
Thou know'st that this cannot be said
A sinne, nor shame, nor losse of maidenhead,
 Yet this enjoyes before it wooe,
 And pamper'd swells with one blood made of two,
 And this, alas, is more than wee would doe.

Oh stay, three lives in one flea spare,
When we almost, nay more than maryed are.
This flea is you and I, and this
Our marriage bed, and marriage temple is;
Though parents grudge, and you, w'are met,
And cloysterd in these living walls of Jet.
 Though use make thee apt to kill me,
 Let not to this, selfe murder added bee,
 And sacrilege, three sinnes in killing three.

Cruell and sodaine, has thou since
Purpled thy naile, in blood of innocence?
In what could this flea guilty bee,
Except in that drop which it suckt from thee?
Yet thou triumph'st, and saist that thou
Find'st not thyself, nor mee the weaker now;
 'Tis true, then learne how false, feares bee;
 Just so much honor, when thou yeeld'st to mee,
 Will wast, as this flea's death tooke life from thee.

John Donne, 'The Flea' (1633)

I'll not weep that thou art going to leave me,
There's nothing lovely here;
And doubly will the dark world grieve me,
While thy heart suffers there.

I'll not weep, because the summer's glory
Must always end in gloom;
And, follow out the happiest story —
It closes with a tomb!

And I am weary of the anguish
Increasing winters bear;
Weary to watch the spirit languish
Through years of dead despair.

So, if a tear, when thou art dying,
Should haply fall from me,
It is but that my soul is sighing,
To go and rest with thee.

Emily Bronte, 'Stanzas' (1846)

I tell you, hopeless grief is passionless;
That only men incredulous of despair,
Half-taught in anguish, through the midnight air
Beat upward to God's throne in loud access
Of shrieking and reproach. Full desertness,
In souls as countries, lieth silent-bare
Under the blanching, vertical eye-glare
Of the absolute Heavens. Deep-hearted man, express
Grief for thy Dead in silence like to death —
Most like a monumental statue set
In everlasting watch and moveless woe
Till itself crumble to the dust beneath.
Touch it; the marble eyelids are not wet:
If it could weep, it could arise and go.

Elizabeth Barrett Browning, 'Grief' (1862)

Prose passages

Knotted at her throat she wore a lilac scarf that even in the achromatic sunshine cast its color up to her face and down around her moving feet in a lilac shadow. Her face was hard, almost stern, save for the soft gleam of piteous doubt that looked from her green eyes. Her once fair hair had darkened, but she was lovelier now at twenty-four than she had been at eighteen, when her hair was brighter than she.

Following a walk marked by an intangible mist of bloom that followed the white border stones she came to a space overlooking the sea where there were lanterns asleep in the fig trees and a big table and wicker chairs and a great market umbrella from Sienna, all gathered about an enormous pine, the biggest tree in the garden. She paused there a moment, looking absently at a growth of nasturtiums and iris tangled at its foot, as though sprung from a careless handful of seeds, listening to the plaints and accusations of some nursery squabble in the house. When this died away on the summer air, she walked on, between kaleidoscopic peonies massed in pink clouds, black and brown tulips and fragile mauve-stemmed roses, transparent like sugar flowers in a confectioner's window — until, as if the scherzo of color could reach no further intensity, it broke off suddenly in mid-air, and moist steps went down to a level five feet below.

Here there was a well with the boarding around it dank and slippery even on the brightest days. She went up the stairs on the other side and into the vegetable garden; she walked rather quickly; she liked to be active, though at times she gave an impression of repose that was at once static and evocative. This was because she knew few words and believed in none, and in the world she was rather silent, contributing just her share of urbane humor with a precision that approached meagreness. But at the moment when strangers tended to grow uncomfortable in the presence of this economy she would seize the topic and rush off with it, feverishly surprised with herself — then bring it back and relinquish it abruptly, almost timidly, like an obedient retriever, having been adequate and something more.

F. Scott Fitzgerald, *Tender is the Night* (1939 revised edn)

About this time there drove up to an exceedingly snug and well-appointed house in Park Lane, a travelling chariot with a lozenge on the panels, a discontented female in a green veil and crimped curls on the rumble, and a large and confidential man on the box. It was the equipage of our friend Miss Crawley, returning from Hants. The carriage windows were shut; the fat spaniel, whose head and tongue ordinarily lolled out of one of them, reposed on the lap of the discontented female. When the vehicle stopped, a large round bundle of shawls was taken out of the carriage by the aid of various domestics and a young lady who accompanied the heap of cloaks. That bundle contained Miss Crawley, who was conveyed upstairs forthwith, and put into a bed and chamber warmed properly as for the reception of an invalid. Messengers went off for her physician and medical man. They came, consulted, prescribed, vanished. The young companion of Miss Crawley, at the conclusion of their interview, came in to receive their instructions, and administered those antiphlogistic medicines which the eminent men ordered.

Captain Crawley of the Life Guards rode up from Knightsbridge Barracks the next day; his black charger pawed the straw before his invalid aunt's door. He was most affectionate in his inquiries regarding that amiable relative. There seemed to be much source of apprehension. He found Miss Crawley's maid (the discontented female) unusually sulky and despondent; he found Miss Briggs, her dame de compagnie, in tears alone in the drawing-room. She had hastened home, hearing of her beloved friend's illness. She wished to fly to her couch, that couch which she, Briggs, had so often smoothed in the hour of sickness. She was denied admission to Miss Crawley's apartment. A stranger was administering her medicines — a stranger from the country — an odious Miss … — tears choked the utterance of the dame de compagnie, and she buried her crushed affections and her poor old red nose in her pocket handkerchief.

Rawdon Crawley sent up his name by the sulky femme de chambre, and Miss Crawley's new companion, coming tripping down from the sick-room, put a little hand into his as he stepped forward eagerly to meet her, gave a glance of great scorn at the bewildered Briggs, and beckoning the young Guardsman out of the back drawing-room, led him downstairs into that now desolate dining-parlour, where so many a good dinner had been celebrated.

Here these two talked for ten minutes, discussing, no doubt, the symptoms of the old invalid above stairs; at the end of which period the parlour bell was rung briskly, and answered on that instant by Mr. Bowls, Miss Crawley's large confidential butler (who, indeed, happened to be at the keyhole during the most part of the interview); and the Captain coming out, curling his mustachios, mounted the black charger pawing among the straw, to the admiration of the little blackguard boys collected in the street. He looked in at the dining-room window, managing his horse, which curvetted and capered beautifully — for one instant the young person might be seen at the window, when her figure vanished, and, doubtless, she went upstairs again to resume the affecting duties of benevolence.

William Thackeray, *Vanity Fair* (1847–48)

In the first place, Cranford is in possession of the Amazons; all the holders of houses above a certain rent are women. If a married couple come to settle in the town, somehow the gentleman disappears; he is either fairly frightened to death by being the only man in the Cranford evening parties, or he is accounted for by being with his regiment, his ship, or closely engaged in business all the week in the great neighbouring commercial town of Drumble, distant only twenty miles on a railroad. In short, whatever does become of the gentlemen, they are not at Cranford. What could they do if they were there? The surgeon has his round of thirty miles, and sleeps at Cranford; but every man cannot be a surgeon. For keeping the trim gardens full of choice flowers without a weed to speck them; for frightening away little boys who look wistfully at the said flowers through the railings; for rushing out at the geese that occasionally venture in to the gardens if the gates are left open; for deciding all questions of literature and politics without troubling themselves with unnecessary reasons or arguments; for obtaining clear and correct knowledge of everybody's affairs in the parish; for keeping their neat maidservants in admirable order; for kindness (somewhat dictatorial) to the poor, and real tender good offices to each other whenever they are in distress, the ladies of Cranford are quite sufficient. 'A man,' as one of them observed to me once, 'is *so* in the way in the house!' Although the ladies of Cranford know all each other's proceedings, they are exceedingly indifferent to each other's opinions. Indeed, as each has her own individuality, not to say eccentricity, pretty strongly developed, nothing is so easy as verbal retaliation; but, somehow, good-will reigns among them to a considerable degree.

The Cranford ladies have only an occasional little quarrel, spirited out in a few peppery words and angry jerks of the head; just enough to prevent the even tenor of their lives from becoming too flat. Their dress is very independent of fashion; as they observe, 'What does it signify how we dress here at Cranford, where everybody knows us?' And if they go from home, their reason is equally cogent, 'What does it signify how we dress here, where nobody knows us?' The materials of their clothes are, in general, good and plain, and most of them are nearly as scrupulous as Miss Tyler, of cleanly memory; but I will answer for it, the last gigot, the last tight and scanty petticoat in wear in England, was seen in Cranford — and seen without a smile.

I can testify to a magnificent family red silk umbrella, under which a gentle little spinster, left alone of many brothers and sisters, used to patter to church on rainy days. Have you any red silk umbrellas in London? We had a tradition of the first that had ever been seen in Cranford; and the little boys mobbed it, and called it 'a stick in petticoats'. It might have been the very red silk one I have described, held by a strong father over a troop of little ones; the poor little lady — the survivor of all — could scarcely carry it.

Elizabeth Gaskell, *Cranford* (1853)

My true name is so well known in the records or registers at Newgate, and in the Old Bailey, and there are some things of such consequence still depending there, relating to my particular conduct, that it is not be expected I should set my name or the account of my family to this work; perhaps, after my death, it may be better known; at present it would not be proper, no not though a general pardon should be issued, even without exceptions and reserve of persons or crimes.

It is enough to tell you, that as some of my worst comrades, who are out of the way of doing me harm having gone out of the world by the steps and the string, as I often expected to go, knew me by the name of Moll Flanders, so you may give me leave to speak of myself under that name till I dare own who I have been, as well as who I am.

I have been told that in one of neighbour nations, whether it be in France or where else I know not, they have an order from the king, that when any criminal is condemned, either to die, or to the galleys, or to be transported, if they leave any children, as such are generally unprovided for, by the poverty or forfeiture of their parents, so they are immediately taken into the care of the Government, and put into a hospital called the House of Orphans, where they are bred up, clothed, fed, taught, and when fit to go out, are placed out to trades or to services, so as to be well able to provide for themselves by an honest, industrious behaviour.

Had this been the custom in our country, I had not been left a poor desolate girl without friends, without clothes, without help or helper in the world, as was my fate; and by which I was not only exposed to very great distresses, even before I was capable either of understanding my case or how to amend it, but brought into a course of life which was not only scandalous in itself, but which in its ordinary course tended to the swift destruction both of soul and body.

But the case was otherwise here. My mother was convicted of felony for a certain petty theft scarce worth naming, viz. having an opportunity of borrowing three pieces of fine holland of a certain draper in Cheapside. The circumstances are too long to repeat, and I have heard them related so many ways, that I can scarce be certain which is the right account.

However it was, they all agree in this that my mother pleaded her belly, and being found quick with child, she was respited for about seven months; in which time having brought me into the world, and being about again, she was called down, as they term it, to her former judgment, but obtained the favour of being transported to the plantations, and left me about half a year old; and in bad hands, you may be sure.

This is too near the first hours of my life for me to relate anything of myself but by hearsay; it is enough to mention, that as I was born in such an unhappy place, I had no parish to have recourse to for my nourishment in my infancy; nor can I give the least account how I was kept alive, other than that, as I have been told, some relation of my mother's took me away for a while as a nurse, but at whose expense, or by whose direction, I know nothing at all of it.

Daniel Defoe, *Moll Flanders* (1722)

Emma Woodhouse, handsome, clever, and rich, with a comfortable home and happy disposition, seemed to unite some of the best blessings of existence, and had lived nearly twenty-one years in the world with very little to distress or vex her.

She was the youngest of the two daughters of a most affectionate, indulgent father, and had, in consequence of her sister's marriage, been mistress of his house from a very early period. Her mother had died too long ago for her to have more than an indistinct remembrance of her caresses, and her place had been supplied by an excellent woman as governess, who had fallen little short of a mother in affection.

Sixteen years had Miss Taylor been in Mr Woodhouse's family, less as a governess than a friend, very fond of both daughters, but particularly of Emma. Between *them* it was more the intimacy of sisters. Even before Miss Taylor had ceased to hold the nominal office of governess, the mildness of her temper had hardly allowed her to impose any restraint; and the shadow of authority being now long passed away, they had been living together as friend and friend very mutually attached, and Emma doing just what she liked, highly esteeming Miss Taylor's judgment, but directed chiefly by her own.

The real evils, indeed, of Emma's situation were the power of having rather too much her own way, and a disposition to think a little too well of herself; these were the disadvantages which threatened alloy to her many enjoyments. The danger, however, was at present so unperceived that they did not by any means rank as misfortunes with her.

Sorrow came — a gentle sorrow — but not at all in the shape of any disagreeable consciousness. Miss Taylor married. It was Miss Taylor's loss which first brought grief. It was on the wedding-day of this beloved friend that Emma first sat in mournful thought of any continuance. The wedding over, and the bride-people gone, her father and herself were left to dine together, with no prospect of a third to cheer a long evening. Her father composed himself to sleep after dinner, as usual, and she had then only to sit and think of what she had lost.

The event had every promise of happiness for her friend. Mr Weston was a man of unexceptionable character, easy fortune, suitable age, and pleasant manners; and there was some satisfaction in considering with what self-denying, generous friendship she had always wished and promoted the match; but it was a black morning's work for her. The want of Miss Taylor would be felt every hour of every day. She recalled her past kindness — the kindness, the affection of sixteen years — how she had taught and how she had played with her from five years old — how she had devoted all her powers to attach and amuse her in health — and how nursed her through the various illnesses of childhood. A large debt of gratitude was owing here; but the intercourse of the last seven years, the equal footing and perfect unreserve which had soon followed Isabella's marriage, on their being left to each other, was yet a dearer, tenderer recollection. It had been a friend and companion such as few possessed: intelligent, well-informed, useful, gentle, knowing all the ways of the family, interested in all its concerns, and peculiarly interested in herself, in every pleasure, every scheme of hers — one to whom she could speak every thought as it arose, and who had such an affection for her as could never find fault.

How was she to bear the change? It was true that her friend was going only half a mile from them; but Emma was aware that great must be the difference between a Mrs Weston, only half a mile from them, and a Miss Taylor in the house; and with all her advantages, natural and domestic, she was now in great danger of suffering from intellectual solitude. She dearly loved her father, but he was no companion for her. He could not meet her in conversation, rational or playful.

Jane Austen, *Emma* (1815)

Between the kitchen and the destroyed chapel a door led into an oval-shaped library. The space inside seemed safe except for a large hole at portrait level in the far wall, caused by mortar shell attack on the villa two months earlier. The rest of the room had adapted itself to this wound, accepting the habits of weather, evening stars, the sound of birds. There was a sofa, a piano covered in a grey sheet, the head of a stuffed bear and high walls of books. The shelves nearest the torn wall bowed with the rain, which had doubled the weight of the books. Lightning came into the room too, again and again, falling across the covered piano and carpet.

At the far end were French doors that were boarded up. If they had been open she would have walked from the library to the loggia, then down thirty-six penitent steps past the chapel towards what had been an ancient meadow, scarred now by phosphorus bombs and explosions. The German army had mined many of the houses they retreated from, so most rooms not needed had been sealed for safety, the doors hammered into their frames.

She knew these dangers when she slid into the room, walking into its afternoon darkness. She stood conscious suddenly of her weight on the wooden floor, thinking it was probably enough to trigger whatever mechanism was there. Her feet in dust. The only light poured through the jagged mortar circle that looked onto the sky.

Michael Ondaatje, *The English Patient* (1992)

Key terms

- **Allegory** A literary method of representing abstract ideas as objects or people.

- **Alliteration** A pattern of sounds based on repetition, particularly of consonants at the start of words.

- **Ambiguity** Quite apart from its general meaning, this is an important literary term which focuses on language which has more than one meaning, which, unlike in everyday life, is often the basis of a fruitful complexity.

- **Antithesis** This term is used when writers present opposing ideas to achieve a particular impact.

- **Assonance** As with alliteration, but based on repetition of vowel sounds.

- **Bathos** This term is used when a writer has created an anticlimax by making ridiculous an impact that was intended to be elevated. Sometimes this is done intentionally for comic effect.

- **Blank verse** These are poetic lines which are not rhymed and consist of iambic pentameter (a light syllable followed by a stressed one, five times in a line). Shakespeare made extensive use of this form of verse.

- **Caesura** A clear pause that occurs within a poetic line.

- **Cliché** We use this word in a negative way to refer to words or phrases which have been used many times before.

- **Colloquial** This is used to describe a style which is suitable for relaxed speech rather than formal occasions. In literature, colloquialisms can be used to create a particular impact, perhaps in contrast to the more formal style of other language.

- **Couplet** A pair of rhymed poetic lines.

- **Diction** This term is used to describe the vocabulary chosen for a particular piece of writing. So, formal diction would be used in an official document.

- **Didactic** A work of literature which is described as didactic has a particular 'message' or moral or political viewpoint to convey.

- **Empathy** We feel empathy for characters in a novel or play when we identify with their experiences. Sympathy is similar but suggests a more positive 'siding with' those experiences.

- **Enjambment** This term is used about poetic lines which have no end-stop (full stop or comma). The meaning therefore runs on to the next line.

- **Foregrounding** This term is applied to features in a text which draw attention to themselves and therefore to the process of writing itself, sometimes to point up meaning or subvert expectations (as when a writer plays with the idea of genre).

- **Foot** This is a poetic term for a combination of syllables. When these are repeated in a poetic line, they create the rhythm or metre of the line. One of the most common in English literature is the iambic (see blank verse above).

- **Free verse** This is the most common form in modern verse. It lacks the organisation into metre, rhyme, line length and stanza of 'traditional' poetry, but reflects other poetic qualities which separate it from prose.

- **Ideology** This term refers to a coherent set of beliefs and values which binds a particular group of people together, or at least appears to do so. One can therefore refer to a ruling ideology which is dominant at a particular time or a subversive ideology which aims to undermine that prevailing ethos or set of beliefs. It is generally related to the actual facts of existence, the economic and political realities which have given rise to particular beliefs.

- **Irony** The basic meaning of irony is the distinction between what is directly stated by the words and what is really meant or implied. One way in which this is often shown is by the writer 'setting up' a central character so that we — the reader — know much more about a situation than the character does. Sarcasm is a more obvious version of irony.

- **Onomatopoeia** We use this word when a writer has chosen to use a word or phrase whose sound resembles the meaning, such as 'buzz' or 'hiss'.

- **Oxymoron** We use this word when the writer has put together two words which, as we normally use them, would be opposites, such as 'loud silence'.

- **Paradox** This term is applied to a statement which appears on the surface to be contradictory.

- **Pastoral** Pastoral writing celebrates the countryside, often in a rather idealised way.

- **Personification** We use this term to describe the literary technique of attributing human characteristics to something which is not human.

- **Realism** This is one of those words which seems easy but which is in fact, within the context of literary criticism, a difficult term to pin down. At the basic level it describes a view of writing (and other art forms) which represents what we as audiences can identify as real, lived life. The term is particularly used in relation to the work of nineteenth-century novelists.

- **Rhetoric** A rhetorical style is a manipulative or persuasive style, or — more broadly — writing which aims to make a strong impression on the reader through a particular (sometimes formal or elevated) way of writing.

- **Sonnet** Although the rhyme schemes may differ, the basic form of the sonnet is clear: a single stanza, consisting of fourteen iambic pentameter lines (five repeated iambic feet — see under 'foot' above) with a carefully developed rhyme scheme. There is a strong tradition of love sonnets, some of the most famous of which were written by Shakespeare.

Examinations and assessment

What is the examiner looking for?

Throughout your English literature course, you will be assessed on your *understanding* of what you read and your ability to provide an *organised written response*. When answering questions on an unseen text, the overall assessment follows the same pattern. In addition, however, you need to show that you have the confidence to apply your knowledge and understanding to a passage you have not seen before, and the key skill here is your analysis of the ways in which 'structure, form and language shape meaning in literary texts', as the relevant assessment objective (AO) puts it.

The particular AOs which refer to the unseen element of any specification you are following are highlighted in the lists of assessment objectives below.

The assessment objectives

For those taking A2 examinations in 2009 or retaking examinations based on the present specifications:

- **AO1** Communicate clearly the knowledge, understanding and insight appropriate to literary study, using appropriate terminology and accurate and coherent written expression.
- **AO2i** Respond with knowledge and understanding to literary texts of different types and periods.
- **AO2ii** Respond with knowledge and understanding to literary texts of different types and periods, exploring and commenting on relationships and comparisons between literary texts.
- **AO3** **Show detailed understanding of the ways in which writers' choices of form, structure and language shape meaning.**
- **AO4** Articulate independent opinions and judgements, informed by different interpretations of literary texts by other readers.
- **AO5i** Show understanding of the contexts in which literary texts are written and understood.
- **AO5ii** Evaluate the significance of cultural, historical and other contextual influences on literary texts and study.

For those taking examinations from 2009 (AS) or 2010 (A2):

- **AO1** Articulate creative, informed and relevant response to literary texts, using appropriate terminology and concepts, and coherent, accurate written expression.
- **AO2** **Demonstrate detailed critical understanding in recognising the ways in which structure, form and language shape meaning in literary texts.**
- **AO3** Explore connections and comparisons between different literary texts, informed by interpretations of other readers.
- **AO4** Demonstrate understanding of the significance and influence of the contexts in which literary texts are written and received.

The specifications

A requirement to answer questions on an unseen passage can be included in a specification in a number of different ways. For example:

- Short-answer questions with specific reference to aspects of literature like rhyme and voice. (Edexcel, Unit 1)
- A broad, general question (on structure, form and language or simply the phrase 'Write a commentary') on a single passage. (Edexcel, Unit 3 or the IB)
- A non-fiction passage is set which is related to a set topic you have prepared. You are asked about the ways in which the passage reflects the writer's thoughts and feelings and the ways in which they are expressed. In addition, you are asked how 'typical' this passage is in relation to your reading of the topic. (AQA(A), Unit 1)
- A whole paper which tests your response to a range of unseen texts, all related to a prepared topic. In one question you are asked to make a comparison between two passages of the same genre (say two sonnets). In the other, you are asked to compare two passages from different genres (say from a Shakespeare play and a prose extract). (AQA(A), Unit 3)
- A choice of prepared texts, which in the examination you are required to relate to an unseen passage, chosen from a range of material. (WJEC, Unit 4)
- A whole paper which examines your response to a range of unseen passages. You are asked to attempt a compulsory question on two passages from the same genre (say nineteenth-century fiction) and, in addition, choose one further passage for analysis from one other genre (in this case poetry or drama). (Cambridge Pre-U, paper 3)

Make sure that you know the specific requirements of the unseen element in the specification that you are following.

Examiners' tips

Although the way your response to unseen passages is assessed in the present specifications is sometimes a little different from the approach in many of the new examinations, the comments by examiners are relevant to both.

Relate analysis to meaning

One of the most important aspects of writing a response to an unseen question is the need to relate your analysis of the language, form and structure of the piece to your understanding of the meaning or theme(s).

Above all, you need to:

- avoid giving a checklist of terms and quotations, which really only provides a number of examples
- avoid using separate paragraphs for the presentation of your commentary on the language and on the theme

Use terminology appropriately

AO1 requires candidates to use 'appropriate terminology' when exploring texts. However, you must be careful not just to provide a list. There is no point in simply using exemplification (which can end up with a structure that does nothing more than say 'here is another example of...'), as this reveals little about either your understanding or your powers of analysis.

Avoid narrating and describing

As with all literary study, it can be easy to think you are analysing language when in fact all you are doing is putting what is there into your own words.

Do not 'plod through'

Candidates sometimes think that the best approach is to work through the poem or extract, providing a detailed commentary on everything that occurs to them. This is not a good idea. Apart from anything else, it is a time-consuming way to approach the task and it does not show that you can prioritise between the important and the trivial.

A final word

You can learn to answer the unseen question with confidence through practice, practice and yet more practice. This is true of all aspects of your examinations, but particularly the unseen, because so much of your success will be based on technique. In the examination, you need to work fast and respond to the passage(s) in the way that you have planned to do, with absolutely no last-minute panic about how to approach the question.

In this workbook I have tried to focus your mind on the various stages of preparation that you need to practise. Apply those to the particular demands of your specification — and all will be fine. Good luck!